AF228341

Let's go UNDERGROUND!
Let's travel into the murky, muddy **earth**.
It's **dark** and **damp** down here.

There's no sunshine, no birdsong, and no wind.
But it's a world **BURSTING** with life.

Keep reading to find out more!

To Olive
—B. L.

To Mi and Huy
—X. L.

First published 2025 by Nosy Crow Ltd.
Wheat Wharf, 27a Shad Thames
London, SE1 2XZ, UK

This edition published 2026 by Nosy Crow Inc.
145 Lincoln Road
Lincoln, MA 01773, USA

www.nosycrow.us

ISBN 979-8-88777-233-2

Library of Congress Catalog Card Number 2025949804

Printed in Dongguan, China, following rigorous ethical sourcing standards.

3 5 7 9 10 8 6 4 2

WONDER WORLD

EARTH

The Science of Soil

written by
Ben Lerwill

illustrated by
Xuan Le

nosy crow

This is the EARTH.

It's made up of different LAYERS of rock and metal.

At Earth's center, there's a giant ball made mostly of solid **iron**. It's nearly as **hot** as the surface of the sun. We call it the INNER CORE.

The next layer is called the OUTER CORE. It's as hot as the inner core, but it's **liquid** rather than solid. It's a fiery swirl of iron and nickel.

The thickest layer is called the MANTLE.
It's made of very strong, dense rock.
It's so huge that it makes up
more than 60 percent of
Earth's mass.

MANTLE

The TOP layer is called the CRUST.
It's thinner than the other layers.
Like the mantle, it's made of
different kinds of rock.

CRUST

The CRUST is also home to
the most wonderful layer of all . . .

...the SOIL.

It's the VERY TOP layer of
the CRUST of our planet,
where life thrives.

Close to the surface, the crust becomes
much looser and stickier.

Creepy-crawlies
start to appear.

Roots
stretch
down into
the ground.

Soil forms a layer of earth across nearly every part of every country.
It acts like the world's SKIN. It looks brown and cakey,
and it feels soft and crumbly—BUT WHAT IS IT?

Soil is a jumble of lots of different things.
The two main ingredients are
MINERALS and ORGANIC MATERIAL.

MINERALS are tiny bits of
rock, such as sand or clay.

ORGANIC MATERIAL
is a mix of living things
(like roots and insects)

and

nonliving things
(like fallen leaves
and dead plants).

Soil also contains a LOT
of air and water.

Mix it all together and you've got lovely, mucky, wormy, squirmy soil!

Different parts of the world have different kinds of soil.

It can be **heavy**
and **chalky.**

It can even be
tough and **frosty.**

Temperature, **rainfall,** and different **minerals** all change how
soil **looks** and **feels.** But wherever you go, **soil** contains . . .

...LOTS of LIFE!

This is an EARTHWORM. It's about the size of
your little finger. It has no eyes, ears, or
nose, but it's a real underground
HERO.

When it burrows through the soil,
it helps air and water
to spread underground.

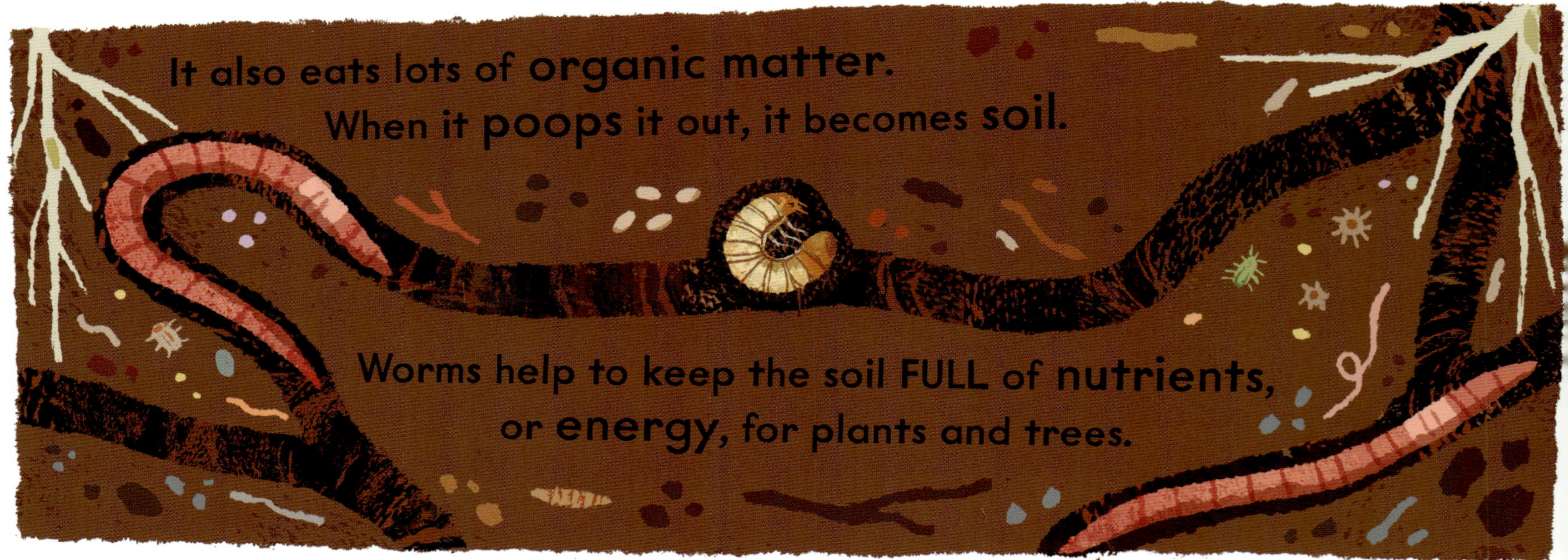

It also eats lots of organic matter.
When it poops it out, it becomes soil.

Worms help to keep the soil FULL of nutrients,
or energy, for plants and trees.

There are many different kinds of worms....

Some WORMS are as **LONG** as a car.

Some are so small they could FIT onto a **freckle**.

Around the world there are

400 BILLION BILLION

worms in the soil!

Worms might be *slippery* and squiggly, but they're also one of the most **important** animals on the planet. As well as helping the soil, they're a VITAL part of . . .

. . . the world's FOOD CHAIN.

BIRDS such as blackbirds, robins, starlings, thrushes, and blue jays **pull UP** worms from the **ground** and **gobble** them up.

MAMMALS such as foxes, warthogs, bears, weasels, and hedgehogs **dig DOWN** into the **soil** to find them.

CREATURES such as beetles, turtles, frogs, snakes, and centipedes all eat **worms**, too.

So, WORMS give the soil more nutrients . . .
the soil gives WORMS a home . . .
and WORMS give animals a meal!

Many other CREEPY-CRAWLIES live **underground**, too.
If you pick up a **clump** of **soil** and look closely,
you'll probably spot LOTS of
TINY CREATURES.

Maybe **millipedes,**

or grubs,

or slimy
slugs.

Maybe
earwigs,

or
termites,

or busy
ants.

In the same handful there are also THOUSANDS and
THOUSANDS of other **creepy-crawlies** . . .

Like worms, these TEENY TINY creatures help
the soil by eating bits of dead plants and roots,
making little gaps where air can spread.
Their poop is GOOD for the soil, too.

Soil also has BILLIONS of even SMALLER living things . . .

. . . called MICROBES.

They're NOT animals. Some MICROBES are BACTERIA, simple things made of just one cell.

Some MICROBES are TINY fungi, sort of like very, VERY SMALL mushrooms.

All MICROBES are so TEENY that you need a special microscope to see them. But they have some VERY important jobs. . . .

Some help things grow by recycling nutrients for plants and crops. Some act as food for TINY creepy-crawlies. Some even make oxygen for us to BREATHE.

Microbes are AMAZING!

And what ELSE lives UNDERGROUND?

About a **third** of all the **animals** in the world **live** UNDERGROUND—and NOT all of them are TINY. . . .

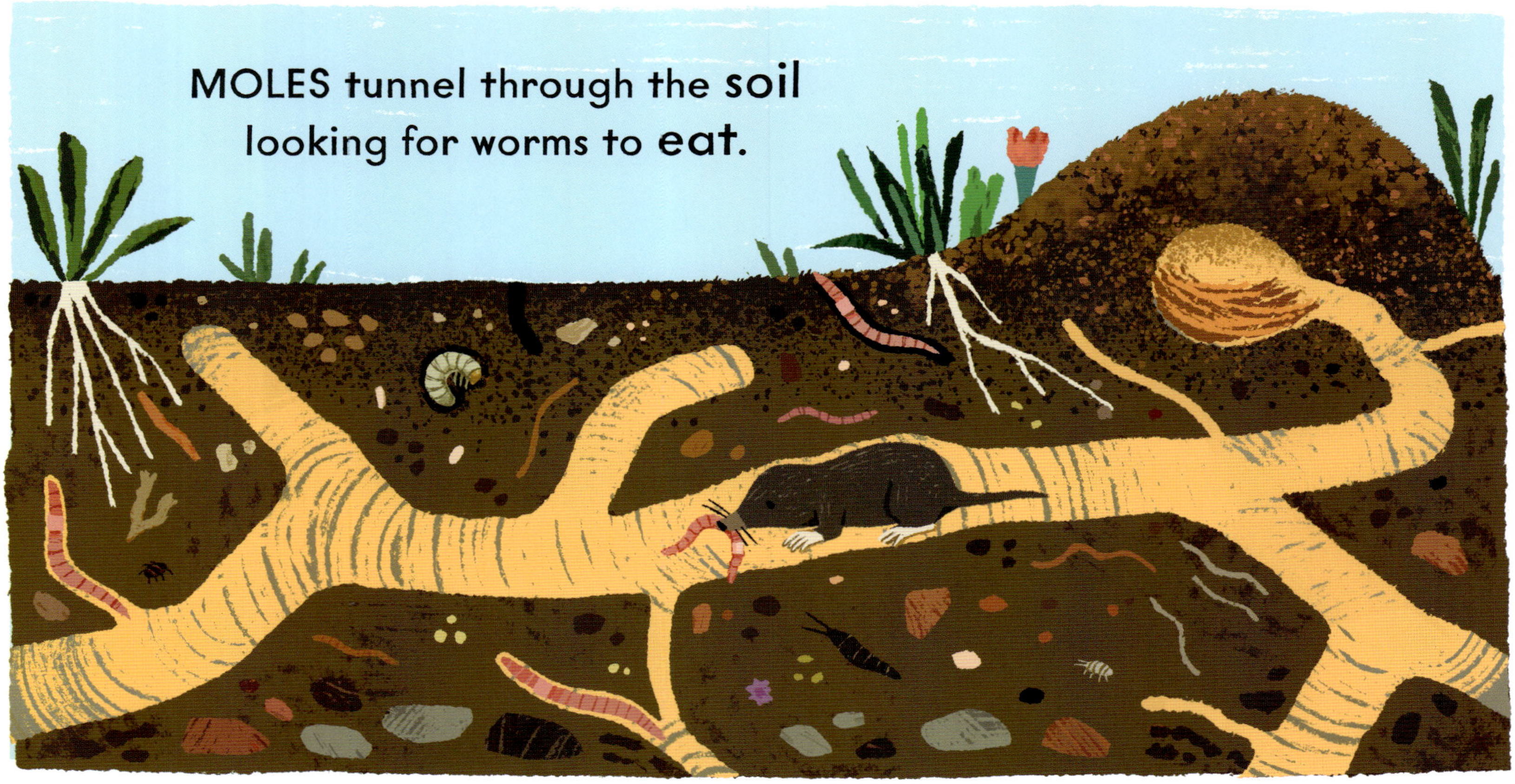

MOLES tunnel through the **soil** looking for worms to **eat**.

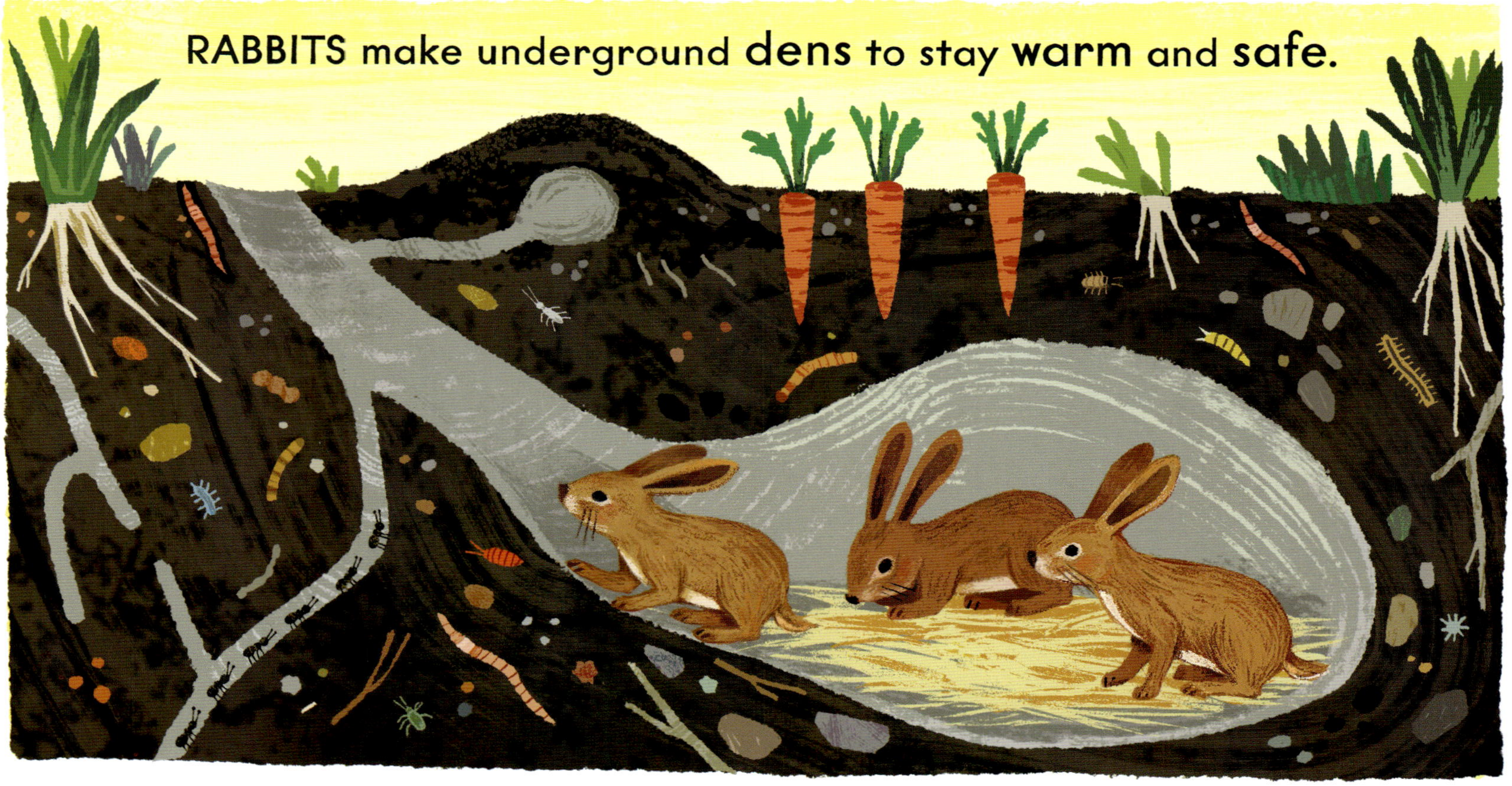

RABBITS make underground **dens** to stay **warm** and **safe**.

PLATYPUSES sleep in **burrows**
near the water's edge.

CHIPMUNKS spend the cold winter
underground, **nesting** and **eating**.

Lots **more** animals live in the **soil.** Can YOU think of any?

When you walk through a FOREST . . .

the **sky** is full of **trunks, branches,** and **leaves.**
But things are even **busier** in the soil!

Underground, the ROOTS of all the trees
and plants spread out like a GIANT web.

Woven through the roots are long, **stringy** strands
of FUNGI, connecting **everything** together. . . .

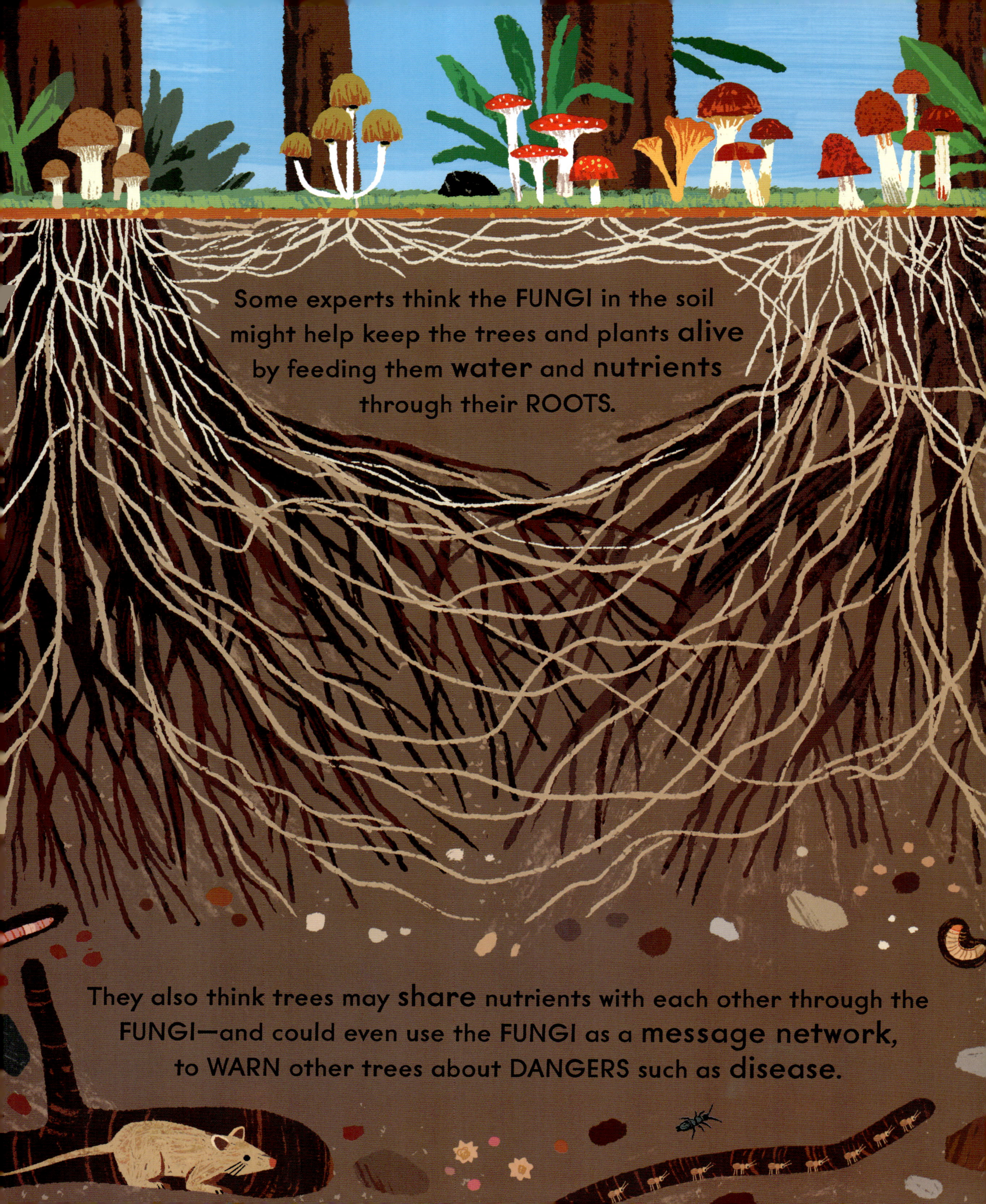

Some experts think the FUNGI in the soil might help keep the trees and plants alive by feeding them water and nutrients through their ROOTS.

They also think trees may share nutrients with each other through the FUNGI—and could even use the FUNGI as a message network, to WARN other trees about DANGERS such as disease.

The whole thing is like an ENORMOUS underground city where everything works **together**: the trees, the roots, the fungi, the microbes, the creepy-crawlies, and the nutrients in the soil!

When **trees**, **roots**, **plants**, and **fungi** die, they DECOMPOSE, or break down into SMALLER pieces . . .

and become part of the **soil**, too.

This brings more **nutrients** to the soil.
This helps MICROBES to **grow**.

The microbes become food for CREEPY-CRAWLIES.
The creepy-crawlies become food for ANIMALS like moles.
Just like trees, roots, and plants, when underground animals die, they DECOMPOSE and become part of the soil, too.
The nutrient-rich soil becomes food for MICROBES.
NATURE IS ALWAYS HARD AT WORK IN THE SOIL!

SOIL gives us OUR food too. . . .

FRUIT TREES and VEGETABLES all need to grow in soil.
Without soil, there would be NO apples, tomatoes,
strawberries, bananas, or cucumbers—or
any other fruits and vegetables!

FARM CROPS need to grow in soil, too. Without soil, there would
be NO bread, pasta, popcorn, chips, rice, chocolate, or sugar.

And because FARM ANIMALS have to **eat** things grown in **soil**,
there would be NO farm animals either. . . .

So there would be NO eggs, butter,
cheese, milk, or meat.

Soil gives us LIFE!

S0IL has other VITAL jobs. . . .

Soil absorbs CARBON DIOXIDE.
  Carbon dioxide is a gas. When we have too much of it in the air,
    it makes the PLANET warmer than it should be.

              By storing carbon dioxide underground,
                healthy soil helps the world to stay at
                      the right TEMPERATURE.

Soil helps support **buildings.** By digging **down** before we build **up,**
houses, schools, and hospitals can stand STRONG.

Soil soaks up rain. Tree and plant ROOTS in the soil
help **stop** water from FLOODING across the ground.

Soil cleans the water too, by helping **absorb** chemicals and bacteria.

All this is happening right **under** our **feet!**

SOIL
is
INCREDIBLE!

It's working day and night,
ALL around the WORLD.

It's alive with TRILLIONS of living things,
all helping to make our planet cleaner and greener.

Without soil,
the world simply wouldn't be
THE WORLD.

So the next time you
pick up a handful of soil,
remember that you're holding . . .

...a muddy, MAGICAL, MARVELOUS MIRACLE!